A YEAR
in the
GARDEN

Annual Planner and Journal

NINA & SONYA MONTENEGRO

Timber Press
Portland, Oregon

Published in 2017 by Timber Press, Inc.
The Haseltine Building
133 S.W. Second Avenue, Suite 450
Portland, Oregon 97204-3527
timberpress.com

Printed in China on paper from responsible sources
Second printing 2022
Text and cover design by Nina & Sonya Montenegro

ISBN: 978-1-60469-828-2

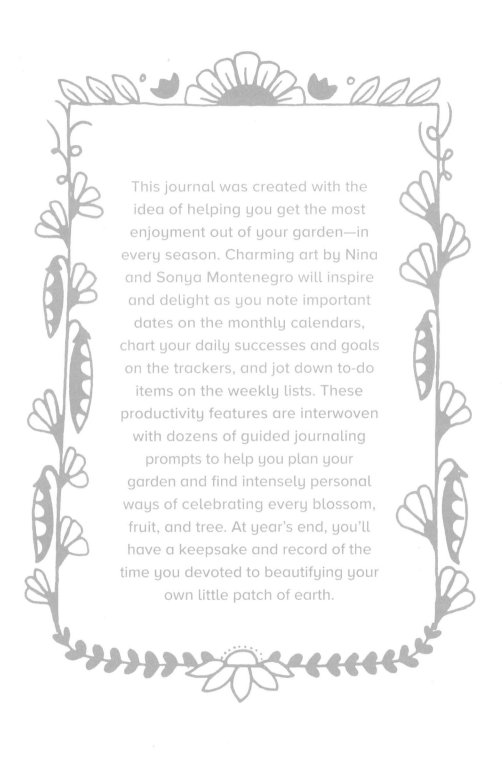

This journal was created with the idea of helping you get the most enjoyment out of your garden—in every season. Charming art by Nina and Sonya Montenegro will inspire and delight as you note important dates on the monthly calendars, chart your daily successes and goals on the trackers, and jot down to-do items on the weekly lists. These productivity features are interwoven with dozens of guided journaling prompts to help you plan your garden and find intensely personal ways of celebrating every blossom, fruit, and tree. At year's end, you'll have a keepsake and record of the time you devoted to beautifying your own little patch of earth.

S	M	T
	1	2
	8	9
	15	16
	22	23
	29	30

JANUARY

W	Th	F	S
3	4	5	6
10	11	12	13
17	18	19	20
24	25	26	27
31			

ACTIVITY OR INTENTION

1 2 3 4 5 6 7

MONDAY

TUESDAY

WEDNESDAY

THURSDAY

FRIDAY

WEEKEND

FEBRUARY

ACTIVITY OR INTENTION

1 2 3 4 5 6 7

FEBRUARY TRACKER

8 9 10 11 12 13 14 15 16 17 18 19 20 21 22 23 24 25 26 27 28 29

MONDAY

TUESDAY

WEDNESDAY

THURSDAY

FRIDAY

WEEKEND

Tools to buy, replace, repair, or maintain:

MONDAY

TUESDAY

WEDNESDAY

THURSDAY

FRIDAY

WEEKEND

Winter may seem like it has no end, but each day brings more light than the day before! Track daylight hours for two weeks.

DATE	SUNRISE	SUNSET

NOTES ABOUT THE QUALITY OF LIGHT

MONDAY

TUESDAY

WEDNESDAY

THURSDAY

FRIDAY

WEEKEND

Fruit trees and deciduous plants in my garden that need pruning:

1.

2.

3.

4.

5.

MONDAY

TUESDAY

WEDNESDAY

THURSDAY

FRIDAY

WEEKEND

Dreaming of this summer's bounty as I'm eating last year's.
Things to plant for preserves:

MONDAY

TUESDAY

WEDNESDAY

THURSDAY

FRIDAY

WEEKEND

MARCH

ACTIVITY OR INTENTION

MARCH TRACKER

8 9 10 11 12 13 14 15 16 17 18 19 20 21 22 23 24 25 26 27 28 29 30 31

MONDAY

TUESDAY

WEDNESDAY

THURSDAY

FRIDAY

WEEKEND

Seedling growth chart:

55

MONDAY

TUESDAY

WEDNESDAY

THURSDAY

FRIDAY

WEEKEND

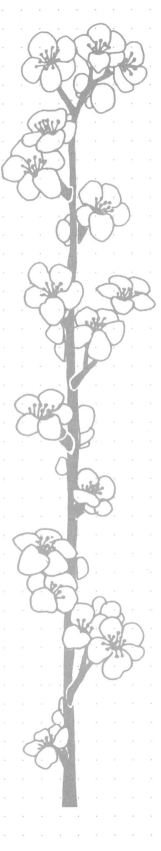

Tend to indoor gardens now—repot any indoor houseplants
that have outgrown their containers. Check for pests.

MONDAY

TUESDAY

WEDNESDAY

THURSDAY

FRIDAY

WEEKEND

Do some spring cleaning for the birds! Get birdhouses ready for the return of feathered friends, or plan where to place new birdhouses in your garden.

Birds I hope to see in my yard this year:

MONDAY

TUESDAY

WEDNESDAY

THURSDAY

FRIDAY

WEEKEND

My favorite trees are beginning to bloom!

DATE   TREE

SKETCH OR DESCRIPTION OF BLOSSOMS

MONDAY

TUESDAY

WEDNESDAY

THURSDAY

FRIDAY

WEEKEND

APRIL

ACTIVITY OR INTENTION

1 2 3 4 5 6 7

APRIL TRACKER

8	9	10	11	12	13	14	15	16	17	18	19	20	21	22	23	24	25	26	27	28	29	30

MONDAY

TUESDAY

WEDNESDAY

THURSDAY

FRIDAY

WEEKEND

Perennials I want to move elsewhere in the garden or divide:

PLANT	MOVE	DIVIDE

GIVE AWAY   COMPOST

MONDAY

TUESDAY

WEDNESDAY

THURSDAY

FRIDAY

WEEKEND

Draw in or list four color combinations you want to create in your garden and the plants that you can group to achieve them.

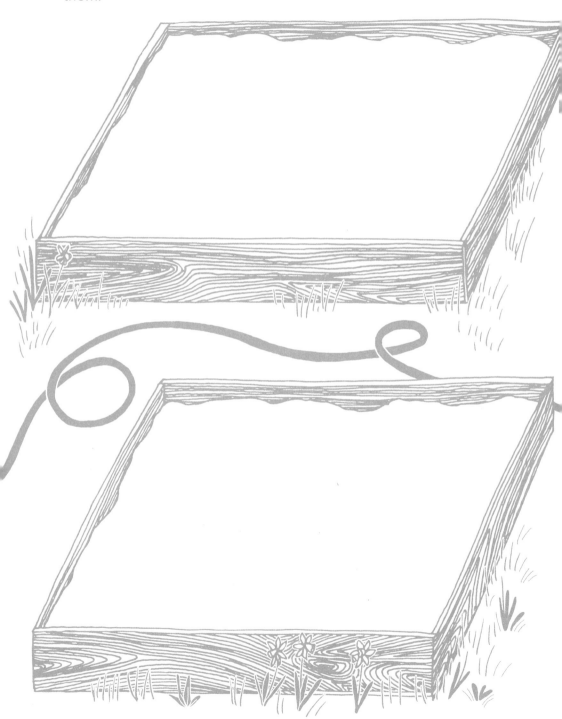

MONDAY

TUESDAY

WEDNESDAY

THURSDAY

FRIDAY

WEEKEND

Trees and shrubs to plant or transplant this year:

MONDAY

TUESDAY

WEDNESDAY

THURSDAY

FRIDAY

WEEKEND

NURSERY
WISHLIST

ANNUALS

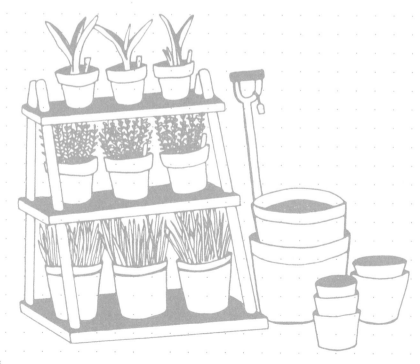

NURSERY WISHLIST

PERENNIALS

MONDAY

TUESDAY

WEDNESDAY

THURSDAY

FRIDAY

WEEKEND

MAY

ACTIVITY OR INTENTION   1 2 3 4 5 6 7

MAY TRACKER

8 9 10 11 12 13 14 15 16 17 18 19 20 21 22 23 24 25 26 27 28 29 30 31

MONDAY

TUESDAY

WEDNESDAY

THURSDAY

FRIDAY

WEEKEND

THREE PETALS

TRILLIUM OVATUM

FOUR PETALS

HESPERIS MATRONALIS

Flowers aren't just for the garden! Celebrate things being back in bloom by finding wildflowers in your neighborhood or nearby nature preserve with three petals, four petals, and five petals—or more. Identify and sketch or describe them.

FIVE PETALS

PHLOX SPECIOSA

MONDAY

TUESDAY

WEDNESDAY

THURSDAY

FRIDAY

WEEKEND

Coveting the neighbor's garden? Note down four good design ideas that you see in a nearby yard that you might like to try in your own.

MONDAY

TUESDAY

WEDNESDAY

THURSDAY

FRIDAY

WEEKEND

Don't forget containers! Draw or fill in what you would like to plant in window boxes or large pots this year.

MONDAY

TUESDAY

WEDNESDAY

THURSDAY

FRIDAY

WEEKEND

Plant late-summer bulbs this month! List those you would like to incorporate into your garden this year, and how many bulbs of each you will need.

GLADIOLA

LILY

CHOCOLATE COSMOS

MONDAY

TUESDAY

WEDNESDAY

THURSDAY

FRIDAY

WEEKEND

JUNE

JUNE TRACKER

ACTIVITY OR INTENTION

1 2 3 4 5 6 7

8 9 10 11 12 13 14 15 16 17 18 19 20 21 22 23 24 25 26 27 28 29 30

MONDAY

TUESDAY

WEDNESDAY

THURSDAY

FRIDAY

WEEKEND

Draw or chart the growth of a vining plant you have in your garden, such as a clematis, ivy, or tomato, noting heights each week and when the flowers or fruits first appear.

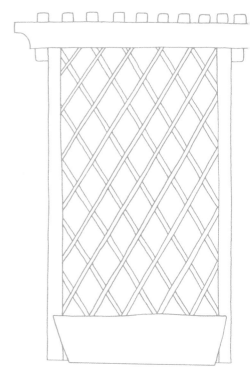

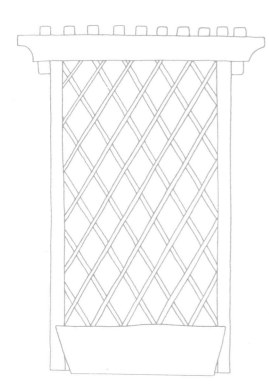

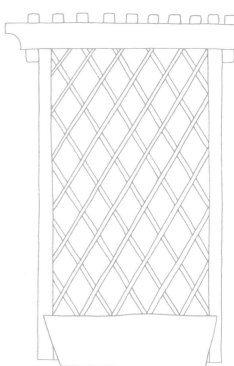

MONDAY

TUESDAY

WEDNESDAY

THURSDAY

FRIDAY

WEEKEND

Bugs, butterflies, birds, and bats make good garden friends.
List or sketch the wildlife your garden is attracting, noting the
time of day you saw each and what plants they seem to like.

BEE

HUMMINGBIRD

WALKING STICK

BUTTERFLY

BEETLE

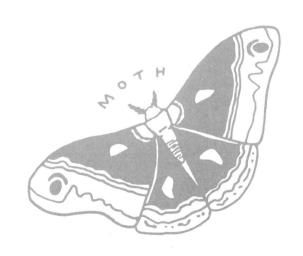

MOTH

MONDAY

TUESDAY

WEDNESDAY

THURSDAY

FRIDAY

WEEKEND

Celebrate the summer solstice by spending the evening in your garden. Sketch or describe how your garden looks or sounds at sunset.

MONDAY

TUESDAY

WEDNESDAY

THURSDAY

FRIDAY

WEEKEND

Draw or describe three flowers that
have appeared in your garden so far this year
that make you the most proud (these could be on
vegetables as well).

MONDAY

TUESDAY

WEDNESDAY

THURSDAY

FRIDAY

WEEKEND

JULY

ACTIVITY OR INTENTION

1 2 3 4 5 6 7

JULY TRACKER

8 9 10 11 12 13 14 15 16 17 18 19 20 21 22 23 24 25 26 27 28 29 30 31

MONDAY

TUESDAY

WEDNESDAY

THURSDAY

FRIDAY

WEEKEND

Meals to make with the bounty from my garden:

MONDAY

TUESDAY

WEDNESDAY

THURSDAY

FRIDAY

WEEKEND

Herbs I planted for flavor or scent:

MONDAY

TUESDAY

WEDNESDAY

THURSDAY

FRIDAY

WEEKEND

GOOSEBERRIES

Bountiful cherries and berries in the garden! Use three words to describe each of the berries you grew or tasted this year.

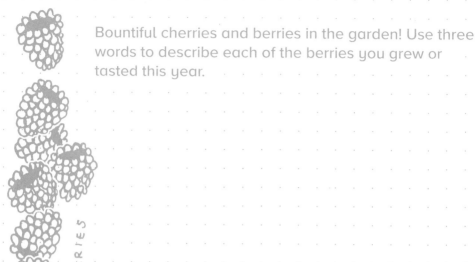

RASPBERRIES

BLUEBERRIES

BLACKBERRIES

CURRANTS

TAYBERRIES

STRAWBERRIES

CHERRIES

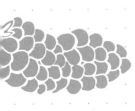

MONDAY

TUESDAY

WEDNESDAY

THURSDAY

FRIDAY

WEEKEND

List or draw the perennials you incorporated into your garden this year.

PURPLE FOUNTAIN GRASS

ECHINACEA

BEE BALM

MONDAY

TUESDAY

WEDNESDAY

THURSDAY

FRIDAY

WEEKEND

AUGUST

ACTIVITY OR INTENTION   1 2 3 4 5 6

AUGUST TRACKER

9 10 11 12 13 14 15 16 17 18 19 20 21 22 23 24 25 26 27 28 29 30 31

MONDAY

TUESDAY

WEDNESDAY

THURSDAY

FRIDAY

WEEKEND

Things to do with all that summer squash:

MONDAY

TUESDAY

WEDNESDAY

THURSDAY

FRIDAY

WEEKEND

Sketch or list the late-summer-blooming perennials in your garden, then list as many alternate common names as you can for them.

MONDAY

TUESDAY

WEDNESDAY

THURSDAY

FRIDAY

WEEKEND

Bulbs to order now for fall planting and spring color, and ideas for planting in succession:

MONDAY

TUESDAY

WEDNESDAY

THURSDAY

FRIDAY

WEEKEND

Create a cold frame planting plan for late fall and winter.

MONDAY

TUESDAY

WEDNESDAY

THURSDAY

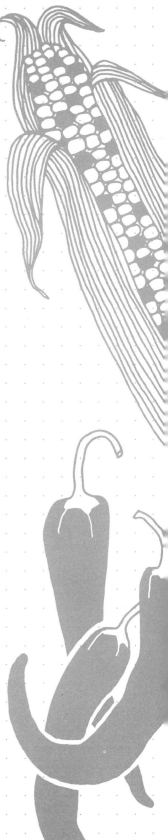

FRIDAY

WEEKEND

SEPTEMBER

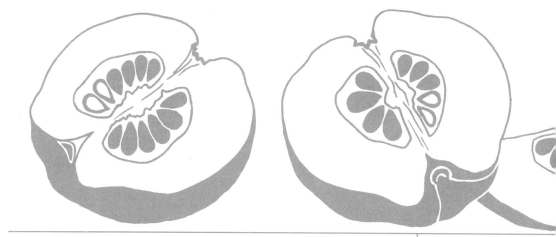

ACTIVITY OR INTENTION

1 2 3 4 5 6 7

SEPTEMBER TRACKER

8 9 10 11 12 13 14 15 16 17 18 19 20 21 22 23 24 25 26 27 28 29 30

MONDAY

TUESDAY

WEDNESDAY

THURSDAY

FRIDAY

WEEKEND

A lot happens in the garden over the course of a day. Observe your garden at intervals and draw or describe changes or differences you see.

6 A.M.   10 A.M.   NOON

2 P.M.   6 P.M.

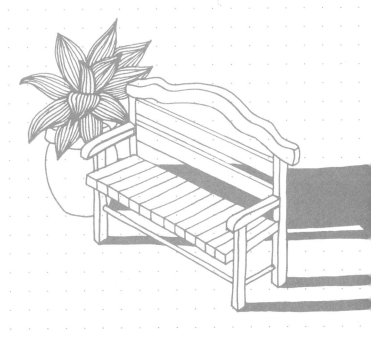

MONDAY

TUESDAY

WEDNESDAY

THURSDAY

FRIDAY

WEEKEND

Celebrate the fertile soil in your garden by grabbing a handful and describing how it feels, smells, and what color it is. See if any insects or worms are in it. List any amendments you made to it this year, what you need to add this fall, or how you plan to change your composting habits in the future.

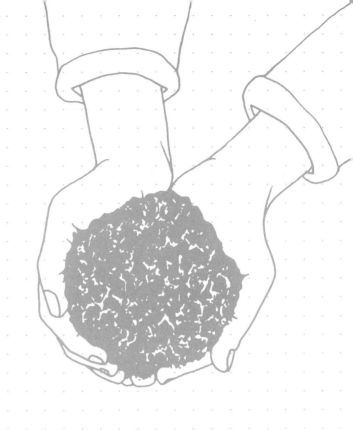

MONDAY

TUESDAY

WEDNESDAY

THURSDAY

FRIDAY

WEEKEND

I'm bringing blooms indoors by forcing these bulbs over the winter:

AMARYLLIS

PAPERWHITE

195

MONDAY

TUESDAY

WEDNESDAY

THURSDAY

FRIDAY

WEEKEND

SPRUCE

JUNIPER BOXWOO

Evergreens to plant or transplant so they will still have
time to root before cold weather sets in:

FIR

CEDAR EUONYMUS

ARBORVITAE CYPR

OLLY camellia FIRETHORN azalea PINE gardenia YEW

MONDAY

TUESDAY

WEDNESDAY

THURSDAY

FRIDAY

WEEKEND

OCTOBER

ACTIVITY OR INTENTION

1 2 3 4 5 6 7

OCTOBER TRACKER

8 9 10 11 12 13 14 15 16 17 18 19 20 21 22 23 24 25 26 27 28 29 30 31

MONDAY

TUESDAY

WEDNESDAY

THURSDAY

FRIDAY

WEEKEND

Recipes for all those root vegetables:

MONDAY

TUESDAY

WEDNESDAY

THURSDAY

FRIDAY

WEEKEND

Draw or describe the plants in your garden that provide the most brilliant fall color, and note peak dates.

SMOKE BUSH

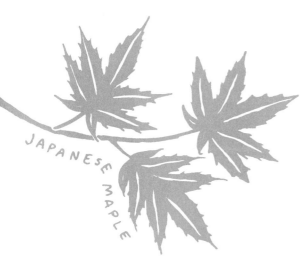

JAPANESE MAPLE

BURNING BUSH

OAKLEAF HYDRANGEA

MONDAY

TUESDAY

WEDNESDAY

THURSDAY

FRIDAY

WEEKEND

Sketch or describe the end-of-season vegetables your garden yielded.

MONDAY

TUESDAY

WEDNESDAY

THURSDAY

FRIDAY

WEEKEND

HONEYCRISP GRAN

Seek out new apple varieties to try at a farmers' market or local apple tasting. Note your new favorites.

CRISPIN BRAEBURN Empire

CORTLAND FUJI

SMITH Jonagold

REDDELICIOUS

gala ROME

tosh ENTERPRISE

MONDAY

TUESDAY

WEDNESDAY

THURSDAY

FRIDAY

WEEKEND

NOVEMBER

ACTIVITY OR INTENTION

1 2 3 4 5 6 7

NOVEMBER TRACKER

8 9 10 11 12 13 14 15 16 17 18 19 20 21 22 23 24 25 26 27 28 29 30

MONDAY

TUESDAY

SIBERIAN IRIS

WEDNESDAY

TURKISH SAGE

THURSDAY

FRIDAY

WEEKEND

TEASEL

NIGELLA

Items from my garden I could use to weave
holiday wreaths for gifts:

MONDAY

TUESDAY

SIBERIAN IRIS

WEDNESDAY

TURKISH SAGE

THURSDAY

FRIDAY

WEEKEND

Dishes I will make for Thanksgiving using produce from my garden:

MONDAY

TUESDAY

SIBERIAN IRIS

WEDNESDAY

TURKISH SAGE

THURSDAY

FRIDAY

WEEKEND

TEASEL

NIGELLA

Draw or describe how your favorite deciduous tree looks now that the leaves are down.

MONDAY

TUESDAY

SIBERIAN IRIS

WEDNESDAY

TURKISH SAGE

THURSDAY

FRIDAY

WEEKEND

TEASEL

NIGELLA

With showier plants finishing their displays for the year, look in your garden for mushrooms, mosses, and lichens. Sketch, describe, and identify them here.

MONDAY

TUESDAY

SIBERIAN IRIS

WEDNESDAY

TURKISH SAGE

THURSDAY

FRIDAY

WEEKEND

TEASEL

NIGELLA

DECEMBER

DECEMBER TRACKER

ACTIVITY OR INTENTION

1 2 3 4 5 6 7

8 9 10 11 12 13 14 15 16 17 18 19 20 21 22 23 24 25 26 27 28 29 30 31

MONDAY

TUESDAY

WEDNESDAY

THURSDAY

FRIDAY

WEEKEND

Draw or describe the evergreen trees and shrubs that are still giving structure to your garden.

MONDAY

TUESDAY

WEDNESDAY

THURSDAY

FRIDAY

WEEKEND

Your garden provides rich patterns and textures, even in the depths of winter. Look for interesting tree bark, exposed rocks, or footprints in the snow and describe or sketch them here.

MONDAY

TUESDAY

WEDNESDAY

THURSDAY

FRIDAY

WEEKEND

Research varieties of poinsettia plants you haven't seen before—there are hundreds! Draw or describe and name them here.

MONDAY

TUESDAY

WEDNESDAY

THURSDAY

FRIDAY

WEEKEND

Gardening wish list:

MONDAY

TUESDAY

WEDNESDAY

THURSDAY

FRIDAY

WEEKEND

Garden design sketches:

Garden design sketches:

Nina and Sonya Montenegro are a sister design
and illustration team living on a small organic farm
outside of Portland, Oregon. Their creative studio,
The Far Woods, produces artworks that serve
as educational tools for reconnection to nature,
food, and community. Their practice crosses
disciplines, including teaching handcraft skills,
beekeeping, and growing food, to work toward an
ecologically viable and socially just future.

ninamontenegro.com
sonyamontenegro.com
thefarwoods.com